Nicholas Lee is a specialist Costs Lawyer, Accredited Mediator, and the Managing Director and founder of Paragon Costs Solutions, a leading costs law practice with offices in Bristol and London. He has specialised exclusively in legal costs since 2001 and is widely recognised for his expertise in complex and high-value civil litigation costs disputes, costs management, detailed assessment proceedings, and strategic litigation funding advice.

Nicholas qualified as an Associate of the Association of Law Costs Draftsmen in 2009, became a Fellow in 2011, and was admitted as a Costs Lawyer in 2011 following the recognition of Costs Lawyers in the Legal Services Act 2007.

Prior to establishing Paragon Costs Solutions in 2011, he worked in-house for a Top 100 law firm, progressing to Director of Costs and Partner. His practice has since advised a broad range of clients including leading national law firms, niche regional law firms, local authorities, insurers, housing providers, and international financial institutions.

A recognised commentator and speaker on civil litigation costs, Nicholas regularly delivers seminars and training on costs law, fixed recoverable costs, proportionality, litigation funding, and housing litigation. He is a member of the LexisNexis Dispute Resolution Expert Panel, a frequent speaker for MBL Seminars and has contributed extensively to legal publications and professional training programmes.

He has particular expertise in housing disrepair costs litigation and frequently advises on complex disputes involving allocation, proportionality, Part 36 strategy and detailed assessment proceedings.

Nicholas is recognised by the leading independent legal directories for his technical expertise and commercial approach to costs litigation. He is ranked by Chambers UK and recognised by The Legal 500 as a leading individual in costs law. In addition to his legal practice, he has served as President of Bristol Law Society and continues to hold a number of advisory and trustee positions within the legal, educational, and charitable sectors.

A Practical Guide to Costs in Housing Disrepair Cases

A Practical Guide to Costs in Housing Disrepair Cases

Nicholas Lee

Costs Lawyer & Mediator

Managing Director of Paragon Costs Solutions

Law Brief Publishing

Published 2026 by Law Brief Publishing, an imprint of Law Brief Publishing Ltd
30 The Parks
Minehead
Somerset
TA24 8BT

www.lawbriefpublishing.com

Paperback: 978-1-918241-39-6

PREFACE

Housing disrepair litigation has become one of the most active and commercially significant areas of civil practice in England and Wales. Over recent years, practitioners have witnessed procedural reform, increasing judicial scrutiny of litigation conduct, and a rapidly evolving costs regime that continues to reshape the way these claims are pursued and defended. Against that background, costs issues are no longer merely ancillary to housing disrepair litigation; they are fundamental to risk management, profitability, settlement strategy, and access to justice.

This book has been written for solicitors and legal professionals who require a detailed and practical understanding of costs in housing disrepair claims. It is intended to bridge the gap between housing law and costs law by examining how the Civil Procedure Rules, Pre-Action Protocol and evolving case law interact in day-to-day practice.

The objective of this book is to provide practitioners with practical guidance capable of immediate application in litigation. Throughout the book, emphasis is placed upon the realities faced by modern practitioners conducting housing disrepair litigation. The analysis is informed by both the procedural framework governing costs and the practical experience of conducting and resolving costs in housing disrepair claims in a demanding and fast-changing litigation environment.

It is hoped that this book will serve as a reliable reference for claimant and defendant practitioners alike, whether acting for tenants, landlords, housing associations, or local authorities. The law and procedure in this area continue to develop at pace, and practitioners must continually adapt their approach to remain both effective and commercially sustainable. If this text assists solicitors in navigating the complexities of costs recovery, reducing litigation risk, and improving the quality of practice within this important field of law, it will have achieved its purpose.

The law stated in this book is believed to be accurate and up to date as at 1st May 2026.

Nicholas Lee
May 2026

DEFINITIONS

This book relates to legal costs in Housing Disrepair Claims in England. Broadly this encompasses residential claims brought under section 11 and/or 9 of the Landlord and Tenant Act 1985 and those brought under the express or implied term of a tenancy agreement.

Unless otherwise stated:

- Tenant may be referred to as the Claimant or receiving party; and

- Landlord may be referred to as the Defendant or paying party.

CONTENTS

CHAPTER ONE

OVERRIDING OBJECTIVE

One cannot consider costs without first having regard to the overriding objective.

The overriding objective of the Civil Procedure Rules ("CPR") is to enable the Courts to deal with cases justly and at proportionate costs.

> *(2) Dealing with a case justly and at proportionate cost includes, so far as is practicable –*
>
> *(a) ensuring that the parties are on an equal footing and can participate fully in proceedings, and that parties and witnesses can give their best evidence;*
>
> *(b) <u>saving expense</u>;*
>
> *(c) dealing with the case in ways which are <u>proportionate</u> –*
>
> *(i) to the amount of money involved;*
>
> *(ii) to the importance of the case;*
>
> *(iii) to the complexity of the issues; and*
>
> *(iv) to the financial position of each party;*
>
> *(d) ensuring that it is dealt with expeditiously and fairly;*

> *(e) allotting to it an appropriate share of the court's resources, while taking into account the need to allot resources to other cases;*
>
> *(f) promoting or using alternative dispute resolution; and*
>
> *(g) enforcing compliance with rules, practice directions and orders.*

This objective extends to the parties. CPR 1.3 provides that the parties are required to help the Court to further the overriding objective.

This overriding objective underpins the Court's case management decision making process and many of the Civil Procedure Rules dealing with costs.

Proportionately and saving expenses is at the heart of the overriding objective, alongside ensuring efficiency and fairness.

CHAPTER TWO

PRE-ACTION PROTOCOL FOR HOUSING CLAIMS (ENGLAND) "PAP"

Housing disrepair claims often give rise to disputes about notice, disclosure, delay and scope of works. The PAP sets out how these claims should be conducted.

Aims of the Protocol

It is important to consider the PAP in the context of costs. After all, one of the aims of the protocol is to keep the costs of resolving disputes down (2.1(f)) which echoes the overriding objective.

Another aim of the protocol is to promote the speedy and appropriate carrying out of any remedial works which is the landlord's responsibility (2.1(b)) which again echoes the overriding objective.

A landlord's liability generally arises once they have received notice of the disrepair. Costs disputes frequently turn on whether notice had been given properly or at all. If the Landlord has not been given notice of the alleged items of disrepair, they will often take issue that a claim has been brought without giving them the opportunity to promptly undertake the necessary remedial works.

There can also be costs disputes arising from Landlords being refused access to carry out the necessary remedial works. This may be driven by costs, as once the remedial works are completed, it may push the claim into the small claims territory (as per *Birmingham v Lee*- see chapter 3). Section 7.6 of the PAP provides that:

> *Tenants must allow the landlord reasonable access for inspection and the carrying out of works in accordance with the tenancy agreement. The landlord should give reasonable notice of the need for access, except in the case of an emergency. The landlord must give access to common parts as appropriate, for example, for the inspection of a shared heating system. If the tenant is no longer in occupation of the premises, the landlord should take all reasonable steps to give access to the tenant for the purpose of an inspection.*

The PAP also provides for the early exchange of information (2.1(d)). Tenants will often request a copy of the tenancy agreement the tenancy file; any documents relating to notice of poor housing conditions given, including copies of any notes of meetings and oral discussions; any inspection reports or documents relating to works required to the property; and any computerised records (as per 5.3 of the PAP).

Alternative Dispute Resolution ("ADR")

ADR is featured in both the overriding objective and PAP.

Landlords often argue that proceedings have been issued prematurely, particularly in circumstances where they have not yet been able to inspect the property, have not yet received expert evidence, or negotiations are ongoing. By contrast, Tenants will often argue that proceedings have been issued due to a lack of progress by the Landlord.

Section 4.1 provides that:

> *The courts take the view that litigation should be a last resort, and that claims should not be issued while a settlement is still actively being explored. Parties should be aware that the court will take into account the extent of the parties' compliance with this Protocol when making orders about who should pay costs.*

Clearly the intention of this warning is to ensure that litigation truly is treated as a last resort and not as a strategy to exert pressure.

Section 4.2 then provides options for resolving the dispute. Mediation is rarely deployed pre-litigation. It is probably the case that mediation is not deemed cost effective for a low-value claim. Instead, Landlords will often encourage Tenant's to pursue their complaints procedures. The issue with complaints procedures is, again, costs. Often it is the case that resolutions under complaints procedures will include specific performance and compensation, but rarely does it include costs. This causes conflict between the Claimant and their solicitors. On the one hand this resolution may be attractive to the Claimant, whose primary goal is for the repairs to be undertaken and to be appropriately compensated. However, the Claimant's solicitor will want to ensure that they are able to recover their costs, often incurred pursuant to a CFA. If a settlement is achieved which does not provide for costs, then the Claimant's solicitor will not be able to recover from the Defendant. Claimant solicitors are therefore in an undesirable position whereby their client's best interests are served by pursuing the complaints procedure, but their own interests are not. It seems that this can be resolved by Claimant solicitors encouraging clients to pursue the Landlord's complaints procedure before a claim is initiated. Such procedures are designed in such a way that a lay person can advance a complaint without legal representation. Indeed, Landlords are more likely to offer more attractive settlement terms if costs are removed from the equation. Importantly, for Landlords, is that they have an effective complaints procedure which encourages and facilitates resolution of potential claims.

Landlords should also be aware of section 6.4 of the PAP. If the Landlord fails to respond to the Letter of Claim within 20 days, or at all, this is a breach of the Protocol and the Tenant is then free to issue proceedings.

Timetable

Step	When
Letter of Claim	Earliest possible opportunity (5.2)
Landlord's Response	20 working days of receipt (6.2)
Single Joint Expert or Joint Inspection	The property should be inspected within 20 working days of the Landlord's Response (7.4)
Single Joint Expert Report or Schedule of Works in the event of a joint inspection	Within 10 working days of the inspection or joint inspection (7.4).
Take stock	Before issuing proceedings (8)

If a Claimant has not engaged in ADR before issuing proceedings, then Defendants may apply for an appropriate stay.

In *Rebecca Jones v Bristol City Council* (7 August 2024 in Bristol County Court) District Judge Wales was considering the costs position when a claim was resolved under a complaints procedure. The Claimant sent a letter of claim on 22 February 2022. The Defendant initiated its Internal Complaints Procedure and alleged that the involvement of lawyers was inappropriate unless and until the complaint procedure had been exhausted. The Claimant proceeded to inspect the property and obtain expert evidence. On 18 April 2023 the Defendant completed its Stage 1 response to the complaint and, whilst denying liability, offered £475 in compensation. The Claimant issued proceedings on 30 March 2023. A defence was filed on 23 June 2023. By consent the claim was stayed for 3 months to enable ADR. On 2 November 2023 the Defendant issued its Stage 2 response under the ICP and offered compensation of £1,502. This was accepted on 10 November 2023. The position of the Claimant at the hearing was that the claim had come to an end by reason of the stage 2 payment by the Defendant to the Claimant, but that the question of costs remained unresolved. The Claimant therefore sought an order for costs up to the date the repairs were completed, relying upon the Court of Appeal judgment in *Birmingham City Council v Lee* [2008] EWCA Civ 891. The Defendant contended that the involvement of lawyers on behalf of the Claimant, sending a letter of claim, and then the issue of proceedings, was not justified in the circumstances of this case, where the matter was resolved by the Defendant's responsive repairs team and the Defendant's internal complaint procedure at stage 2. The Claimant claimed that the involvement of lawyers was justified, in that the Claimant had a fully formed cause of action in relation to the alleged disrepair at the time that the letter of claim was sent, and given the delays in progressing the first stage ICP, the issue of proceedings was justified, and that the second stage of the ICP was not completed in any event until November 2023, some 21 months following the letter of claim, and in any event the result of the ICP included an admission of and compensation for delay. The Court was therefore left to resolve the question of costs without having had the benefit of hearing the case and resolving the dispute of fact and law between the parties. The Court acknowledged the guidance of the

Court of Appeal in *BCT Software Solutions Ltd v Brewer & Sons Ltd* [2003] EWCA Civ 939 which recognised the jurisdiction of the Court to do so. Where it was clear which party was the successful party upon a settlement, the Court may be more willing to determine outstanding issues of costs; however, the Court should be slow to embark upon on the determination of disputed facts solely in order to put the Court in a position to make a decision about costs. The Court should not depart from the normal order unless it is in a clear position to do so on a proper basis of agreed or determined facts which enable the Court to decide what order as to costs ought to be made. There was no presumption that where a dispute is determined without agreement as to costs then the default position was 'no order as to costs'. The Court acknowledged that the protocol does not require the Claimant to attempt or exhaust ADR before issuing a letter of claim, but it did require the parties to consider whether ADR was more suitable than litigation. The Court considered the framework provided by *Birmingham v Lee*. The original complaint was credible and fell within the remit of the fast-track. The works had been completed by 1 June 2023. The proceedings, as issued, did not recognise the works that had been carried out by the Defendant. The final settlement of the claim did not result in any additional works being undertaken. Whilst the Claimant ought to be entitled to its costs up to 1 June 2023, the Claimant had failed to exhaust the complaints procedure before issuing the claim. The Court found that the Claimant should have moved onto the stage 3 of the complaints procedure before issuing proceedings. As such there was scope to criticise the Claimant for prematurely issuing proceedings. Rather than seek to assess the Claimant's reasonable costs on the fast track up until 1 June 2023 and setting those off against the Defendant's assessed costs of the proceedings, the District Judge found that a fair outcome would be that there should be no order as to costs.

Whilst not binding, the above decision is an example of how the Courts may sanction a party which does not comply with the PAP.

There are numerous examples of where parties have been deprived of all or part of their costs for unreasonably refusing to engage in ADR. The leading authority is *Halsey v Milton Keynes General NHS Trust* [2004] EWCA Civ 576 (11 May 2004). This case confirmed that the Court can depart from the usual rule on costs where it can be shown that the successful party has acted unreasonably in refusing ADR:

> *12. CPR 44.3(2) provides that "if the court decides to make an order about costs (a) the general rule is that the unsuccessful party will be ordered to pay the cost of the successful party; but (b) the court may make a different order". CPR 44.3(4) provides that "in deciding what order (if any) to make about costs, the court must have regard to all the circumstances, including-(a) the conduct of the parties". Rule 44.3(5) provides that the conduct of the parties includes "(a) conduct before, as well as during, the proceedings and in particular the extent to which the parties followed any relevant pre-action protocol."*
>
> *13. In deciding whether to deprive a successful party of some or all of his costs on the grounds that he has refused to agree to ADR, it must be borne in mind that such an order is an exception to the general rule that costs should follow the event. In our view, the burden is on the unsuccessful party to show why there should be a departure from the general rule. The fundamental principle is that such departure is not justified unless it is shown (the burden being on the unsuccessful party) that the successful party acted unreasonably in refusing to agree to ADR. We shall endeavour in this judgment to provide some guidance as to the factors that should be considered by the court in deciding whether a refusal to agree to ADR is unreasonable.*

14. *We make it clear at the outset that it was common ground before us (and we accept) that parties are entitled in an ADR to adopt whatever position they wish, and if as a result the dispute is not settled, that is not a matter for the court. As is submitted by the Law Society, if the integrity and confidentiality of the process is to be respected, the court should not know, and therefore should not investigate, why the process did not result in agreement.*

15. *We recognise that mediation has a number of advantages over the court process. It is usually less expensive than litigation which goes all the way to judgment, although it should not be overlooked that most cases are settled by negotiation in the ordinary way. Mediation provides litigants with a wider range of solutions than those that are available in litigation: for example, an apology; an explanation; the continuation of an existing professional or business relationship perhaps on new terms; and an agreement by one party to do something without any existing legal obligation to do so. As Brooke LJ pointed out in Dunnett at para [14]:*

> *"Skilled mediators are now able to achieve results satisfactory to both parties in many cases which are quite beyond the power of lawyers and courts to achieve. This court has knowledge of cases where intense feelings have arisen, for instance in relation to clinical negligence claims. But when the parties are brought together on neutral soil with a skilled mediator to help them resolve their differences, it may very well be that the mediator is able to achieve a result by which the parties shake hands at the end and feel that they have gone away having settled the dispute on terms with which they are happy to live. A mediator may be able*

to provide solutions which are beyond the powers of the court to provide."

16. *In deciding whether a party has acted unreasonably in refusing ADR, these considerations should be borne in mind. But we accept the submission made by the Law Society that mediation and other ADR processes do not offer a panacea, and can have disadvantages as well as advantages: they are not appropriate for every case. We do not, therefore, accept the submission made on behalf of the Civil Mediation Council that there should be a presumption in favour of mediation. The question whether a party has acted unreasonably in refusing ADR must be determined having regard to all the circumstances of the particular case. We accept the submission of the Law Society that factors which may be relevant to the question whether a party has unreasonably refused ADR will include (but are not limited to) the following: (a) the nature of the dispute; (b) the merits of the case; (c) the extent to which other settlement methods have been attempted; (d) whether the costs of the ADR would be disproportionately high; (e) whether any delay in setting up and attending the ADR would have been prejudicial; and (f) whether the ADR had a reasonable prospect of success. We shall consider these in turn. We wish to emphasise that in many cases no single factor will be decisive, and that these factors should not be regarded as an exhaustive checklist.*

What is commonly referred to as the "Halsey test" emerged which was that the Court should consider:

1. The nature of the dispute

2. The merits of the case

3. Other settlement methods that have been attempted

4. The cost of mediation

5. Delay

6. Whether mediation has a reasonable prospect of success

By way of an example, in *Wales (t/a Selective Investment Services) v CBRE Managed Services Ltd & Anor* [2020] EWHC 1050 (Comm) (30 April 2020) the Court deprived the winning Defendant of 50% of its costs for refusing ADR.

The Court of Appeal in *Churchill v Merthyr Tydfil County Borough Council* [2023] EWCA Civ 1416 (29 November 2023) considered whether the Court could lawfully order proceedings to be stayed and for parties to engage in an ADR process. The Court of Appeal concluded that it was lawful to stay existing proceedings and order the parties to engage in a non-Court based dispute resolution process.

Summary

Proper compliance with the PAP is likely to reduce costs and lead to claims being resolved more efficiently. Non-compliance with the PAP is likely to increase costs and give rise to costs sanctions. A winning party could be deprived of part or all of its costs for not complying with the PAP and/or refusing to engage in ADR.

CHAPTER THREE

ALLOCATION & NON-ALLOCATION

General principles

The allocation of the claim, once Court proceedings are issued, can have a significant impact on the amount of recoverable costs. Allocation hearings are often hard fought due to the costs implications.

Costs in housing claims allocated to the fast or multi-track will be assessed having regard to reasonableness and proportionality. Where applicable, the Court will also have regard to the parties last approved or agreed costs budget.

Whilst most civil claims valued up to £100,000, and issued after 1 October 2023, are captured by the Fixed Recoverable Costs (FRC) regime (governed by CPR 45- sections VI and VII), housing condition claims are presently exempt until at least October 2028.

CPR 45.1(4) provides that Sections VI and VII do not apply to a claim or counterclaim which relates, in whole or in part, to a residential property or dwelling and which, in respect of that property, includes a claim for disrepair.

Whilst there are some restrictions where a claim is allocated to the fast-track, such as fixed trial advocacy fees, the majority of the costs are subject to assessment. The main difference between costs on the fast and multi-track, is that fast-track costs are usually summarily assessed following the trial whereas costs awards after a multi-track trial would usually be subject to detailed assessment.

Where housing disrepair claims are allocated to the small claims track, the recoverable costs are very limited. There are often hard-fought hearings as to whether a claim should be allocated to the small claims track or the fast-track.

CPR 27.1 provides that the small claims track is the usual track for any claim which includes a claim by a tenant of residential premises against his landlord for repairs or other work to the premises where the estimated cost of the repairs or other work is not more than £1,000 and the financial value of any other claim for damages is not more than £1,000.

This is reaffirmed in CPR 26.9 which provides that:

> *(1) The small claims track is the normal track for—*
>
> ...
>
> > *(b) any claim which includes a claim by a tenant of residential premises against a landlord where—*
> >
> > > *(i) the tenant is seeking an order requiring the landlord to carry out repairs or other work to the premises (whether or not the tenant is also seeking some other remedy);*
> > >
> > > *(ii) the cost of the repairs or other work to the premises is estimated to be not more than £1,000; and*
> > >
> > > *(iii) the value of any other claim for damages is not more than £1,000; ...*

(5) Subject to paragraphs (6) and (10), the fast track is the normal track for any claim—

(a) for which the small claims track is not the normal track; and (b) which—

(i) is a claim for monetary relief, the value of which is not more than £25,000; or

(ii) is or includes a claim for non-monetary relief and—

(aa) if the claim includes a claim for monetary relief, the value of the claim for monetary relief is not more than £25,000; (bb) the claim meets the criteria in paragraph (6)(a) and (b); and (cc) the court is satisfied that it is in the interests of justice for it to be allocated to the fast track.

This is echoed by PD 7A at paragraph 3.6 which states:

***3.6** If a claim for housing disrepair which includes a claim for an order requiring repairs or other work to be carried out by the landlord is started in the County Court, the claim form must state—*

(1) whether or not the cost of the repairs or other work is estimated to be more than £1000, and

(2) whether or not the claimant expects to recover more than £1000 in respect of any claim for damages.

If either of the amounts mentioned in (1) and (2) is more than £1000, the small claims track will not be the normal track for that claim.

Further assistance on the Court's discretion and the factors to be taken into account can be found at CPR 26.12 and CPR 23.13.

> *26.12.—(1) In considering whether to allocate a claim to the normal track for that claim under rules 26.9, 26.10 or 26.11, the court shall have regard to the matters mentioned in rule 26.13(1).*
>
> *(2) The court must not allocate a claim to the small claims track, if it includes a claim by a tenant of residential premises against his landlord for a remedy in respect of harassment or unlawful eviction.*
>
> *(3) In claims under the Renting Homes (Wales) Act 2016, the court must not allocate a claim to the small claims track if it includes a claim by a contract-holder of a dwelling against their landlord for a remedy in respect of harassment or unlawful eviction.*
>
> ....
>
> *26.13.—(1) When deciding the track for a claim, the matters to which the court shall have regard include—*
>
> *(a) the financial value, if any, of the claim;*
>
> *(b) the nature of the remedy sought;*
>
> *(c) the likely complexity of the facts, law or evidence;*
>
> *(d) the number of parties or likely parties;*
>
> *(e) the value of any counterclaim or additional claim and the complexity of any matters relating to it;*

(f) the amount of oral evidence which may be required;

(g) the importance of the claim to persons who are not parties to the proceedings;

(h) the views expressed by the parties; and

(i) the circumstances of the parties.

(2) It is for the court to assess the financial value of a claim and in doing so it shall disregard—

(a) any amount not in dispute;

(b) any claim for interest;

(c) costs;

(d) any contributory negligence; and

(e) where the claim is, or includes a claim for non-monetary relief, any amount prescribed by rule 45.45(1)(a)(ii) and rule 45.50(2)(b)(ii).

(3) Where—

(a) two or more claimants have started a claim against the same defendant using the same claim form; and

(b) each claimant has a claim against the defendant separate from the other claimants,

the court shall consider the claim of each claimant separately when it assesses financial value under paragraph (1).

What the rules demonstrate is a 2-stage process in which the Court should firstly consider the normal track (stage 1) and then apply the factors at CPR 23.13 (stage 2).

If a housing claim is allocated to the small claims track, then the recoverable costs are limited by Practice Direction 27A which provides that:

> *7.2 The amount which a party may be ordered to pay under rule 27.14(2)(b) (for legal advice and assistance in claims including an injunction or specific performance) is a sum not exceeding £260.*
>
> *7.3(2) for experts' fees, a sum not exceeding £750 for each expert.*

Where a claim is allocated to the small claims track, the recoverable costs remain subject to assessment, but would be limited to £1010 (up to £260 for profit costs and up to £750 for the expert report) excluding VAT.

Unallocated claims

Whilst allocation arguments are commonplace on issued claims, they also extend to cases which settle pre-allocation.

CPR 46.13(3) provides that where the Court is assessing costs on the standard basis of a claim which concludes without being allocated to a track, it may restrict those costs to costs that would have been allowed on the track to which the claim would have been allocated if allocation had taken place.

The Court of Appeal in *Voice & Script International Ltd v Alghafar* [2003] EWCA Civ 736 stated that the principle of proportionality must be considered whenever awards of costs are made and that the Court could consider it reasonable to make an assessment within the small claims costs regime or to apply the regime where that was plainly the correct track. In that case the claim was pleaded at £9,140 which was substantially in excess of the small claims figure (then £5,000). At a disposal hearing on 13 June 2021, the District Judge awarded the Claimant £4,002.43 in damages, plus interest of £755.04 and costs of £6,000. On appeal, His Honour Judge Oppenheimer, reduced the damages to £2,502.43 with a consequential reduction to interest to £470. He also reduced the recoverable costs up to the disposal hearing to £5,000. The paying party appealed the judgment of His Honour Judge Oppenheimer.

The Court of Appeal took the view that £4,002.54, plus interest, represented the fullest possible value of any claim arising in these proceedings. That sum was half the original claim and below the small claims threshold which was then £5,000 (now £10,000). Lord Justice Judge found that:

> *If the issue of allocation had been addressed on the basis of that valuation [£4,002.54] allocation to the small claims track would have been inevitable. The claim was a perfectly straightforward case falling within Part 26.6.3. If so, the successful party's entitlement to costs on the basis of an order in its favour would have been subject to the limitations in part 27.14(2), in particular paragraphs (a) and (d) and 27.14(3).*

Whilst the claim was never allocated to a track, by treating the absence of allocation to track as conclusive, the District Judge misdirected himself. Lord Justice Judge said:

> *The omission may have meant that the small claims costs regime did not follow as a virtually automatic starting point,*

> *but it did not preclude the court even from considering whether it would be reasonable to make an assessment consistent with the small costs regime or, for that matter, to apply the regime to a claim which should never have exceeded and never was anything more than a small claim*

Lord Justice Judge went on to find that:

> *In my view in the absence of any specific factors suggesting otherwise, in a case like this where, if sought, an allocation would have been made to small claims track the normal rule should be that small claims costs regime for costs should apply. While respecting Judge Oppenheimer's hesitation about interfering with a decision which he personally would not have reached, in my judgment he should have done so on the basis of the misdirection which I have identified*

Accordingly, the appeal was allowed, the appellant was awarded £3,000 in respect of the costs of the appeal, and the question of costs up to and including the disposal hearing on 13 June 2021 was remitted to the District Judge for decision.

Voice & Script International Ltd was considered in the Court of Appeal decision of *O'Beirne v Hudson* [2010] EWCA Civ 52 (09 February 2010). In this appeal the question was whether, where a case had been settled before any allocation by a consent order ordering costs to be paid on the standard basis, the costs judge was entitled to take the view that the case would have been allocated to the small claims track and thus that the paying party should only pay costs on the small claims track basis. Lord Justice Waller said:

> *16. In my view, despite the attractive argument of Mr Williams, the answer to this case is straightforward. This was a consent order providing for costs to be assessed on the*

standard basis; the addition of the words reasonable to my mind adds nothing to the order that costs were to be assessed on that basis. It certainly follows from that that the costs judge was not free to rule that the costs would be assessed on the small claims track basis and if and in so far as Judge Stewart might be understood to be saying that he was in my view wrong. But, and this is the critical point, in making an assessment the Costs Judge is entitled to take account of all circumstances (see CPR 44.5(1)), including the fact that the case would almost certainly have been allocated to a small claims track if it had been allocated. In so doing she would have regard to what could or could not be recovered if the case had been so allocated.

17. At that stage the Costs Judge must question whether, if it could have been fought on the small track, it is reasonable that the paying party should pay the costs of a lawyer. The Costs Judge would not be bound (as I think Mr Morgan's formulation would suggest) only to allow the costs as per a case on the small claims track but it would be a highly material circumstance in considering what by way of assessment should be payable.

....

19. I have quoted the passage from Judge LJ's judgment in Voice and Script above. I accept that what was under consideration in that case was what order a trial judge should make when making an order for costs. Thus in many cases the problem that occurred in this case will not arise because the trial judge can actually make an order that costs be assessed on a small claims track basis. I also accept that as Judge Stewart noted, a costs judge has no power to alter the order for costs made by the a judge, and thus make a direction from

> *the outset where costs have been awarded on the standard basis that costs will be assessed on a small track basis. But what lay behind what Judge LJ said reflects what Lord Woolf was saying in Lownds and provided the Costs Judge does not purport to vary the original order or tie himself to assessing by reference to the small claims track it is quite legitimate to give effect as far as possible to the philosophy which lies behind the above statements. There is a real distinction between directing at the outset that nothing but small claims costs will be awarded and giving items on a bill very anxious scrutiny to see whether costs were necessarily or reasonably incurred, and thus whether it is reasonable for the paying party to pay more than would have been recoverable in a case that should have been allocated to the small claims track. Was it for example necessary to have had lawyers and is it reasonable for the paying party to have to pay for lawyers are questions that should arise where a claim should have been allocated to the small claims track.*

Both cases were considered by Costs Judge Nagalingam in *Smith v Wigan Borough Council* [2026] EWHC 660 (SCCO) (18 March 2026). In this case, the value of the repairs was less than £1,000 and the agreed damages were £1,000, settled by way of a Part 36 offer. The Defendant contended that the claim would have been allocated to the small claims track by reference to the agreed damages and the value of the repairs. The Claimant contended that the value of the Claimant's claim for damages was more than £1,000. The Court observed that CPR 29.9(1)(b) refers to the value of the claim for damages, not the agreed amount. The settlement sum may be one measure of value, but it is not definitive. Having regard to the facts of this case, the history of the Claimant's offers which exceeded £1,000 and the Claimant's vulnerability, the Costs Judge concluded that had proceedings been issued, the claim would not have been allocated to the small claims track. Furthermore, the Claimant accepted an offer where the

Defendant inferred no intention to argue costs on the basis of allocation to the small claims track. Accordingly the Claimant was not limited to costs under the small claims track.

Birmingham City Council v Lee [2008] EWCA Civ 891 (30 July 2008)

The case, commonly referred to as *Birmingham v Lee*, deals with the situation where specific performance was sought at the outset but is completed before the claim is concluded. The problem arises because there is a marked difference between the costs recoverable in a case allocated to the small claims track and those recoverable in a case allocated to the fast track.

The Claimant sent a letter of claim on 16 August 2006. The Council inspected the property within a week, and within a month had carried out the great majority of the repairs sought. Proceedings were issued in April 2007, by which point there was no claim for specific performance. The damages sought were pleaded at £1000 – £5000. Liability was disputed as the Council contended it has no sufficient prior notice of the want of repair. The parties filed allocation questionnaires. The parties both agreed that the action fell to be allocated to the small claims track. However, the tenant sought an order for costs on the fast track until at least the date that repairs were completed.

The Deputy District Judge declined to make the order sought by the Claimant. On appeal, Judge MacDuff KC did make an order in relation to pre-allocation costs. The Council appealed to the Court of Appeal.

At paragraph 34 the Court of Appeal said:

> *"Without some order as to the early-incurred costs, it would be open to a landlord who is in fact and in law liable for want of repairs to adopt a deliberate policy of omitting to repair until the protocol letter is received, but then of repairing without admission of liability so as to ensure that any subsequent court claim fell to the small claims track. The result of that would be that fast track costs which would otherwise have been due to the tenant would no longer be payable. We do not say that this is what has happened here; it may well not be. But that very possible scenario illustrates the necessity for some order in relation to the costs of advancing the protocol claim. Moreover, quite independently of the possibility of any such deliberate manipulation of the process by a landlord, such an order is necessary if the protocol is not to operate as a means of preventing recovery of reasonably incurred costs. The tenant who has a justifiable claim for disrepair needs legal assistance in advancing it. He must initiate it in accordance with the protocol. If the effect of the claim is to get the work done, then providing that the landlord was liable for the disrepair the tenant ought to recover the reasonable costs of achieving that result."*.

At paragraph 35 the Court also stated:

> *"...The court's powers are unrestricted in relation to pre-allocation costs. It is, we are satisfied, perfectly proper to make an order in relation to them under CPR 44.9(2) if to do so is necessary in order to ensure that the protocol does not operate to prevent recovery of costs reasonably incurred in achieving the repair."*

The Court concluded at paragraph 36 that:

"... What is necessary in a case of this kind is that the claimant should, providing she is right about liability, recover the reasonable fast-track costs of advancing the claim by way of letter under the protocol, and thus getting the work done. In this case the work was completed by 26 September 2006. We would accordingly replace the order made by the judge with the following:

"Pursuant to CPR 44.9(2), the claimant shall have her costs in the cause on the fast track basis up to 26 September 2006.""

That means that if she wins, she will have fast-track costs of making the claim up to that date. If she fails, she will have nothing. Any costs order, in favour of either side, relating to the period after 26 September will remain governed by the allocation to the small claims track. The certain knowledge that that order will stand if she succeeds can inform any efforts to settle. In future cases of a similar kind, the expectation of an order such as this should have a similar effect, and it is to be hoped, without the need for litigation beyond the protocol negotiations.

CPR 44.9(2), at the time of Birmingham City Council v Lee, was as follows:

"Once a claim is allocated to a particular track, those special rules shall apply to the period before, as well as after, allocation except where the court or a practice direction provides otherwise".

The Civil Procedure (Amendment) Rules 2013 revoked this rule with effect from 1 April 2013, and a new rule was introduced on this date (CPR 46.13(2)):

> *"Where—*
>
> > *(a) claim is allocated to a track; and*
> >
> > *(b) the court subsequently re-allocates that claim to a different track,*
> >
> > *then unless the court orders otherwise, any special rules about costs applying—*
> >
> > > *(i) to the first track, will apply to the claim up to the date of re-allocation; and*
> > >
> > > *(ii) to the second track, will apply from the date of re-allocation".*

Such a new rule was then revoked by the Civil Procedure (Amendment No 2) Rules 2023 on 1 October 2023. What remains of relevance in this regard is within CPR 46.13(1):

> *"Any costs orders made before a claim is allocated will not be affected by allocation".*

CPR PD 46 also sets out at paragraph 7.1(3):

> *"Where a claim, issued for a sum in excess of the normal financial scope of the small claims track, is allocated to that track only because an admission of part of the claim by the defendant reduces the amount in dispute to a sum within the normal scope of that track; on entering judgment for the admitted part before allocation of the balance of the claim the court may allow costs in respect of the proceedings down to that date"*

Birmingham v Lee remains the lead authority for the notion that fast track costs may be awarded in situations where specific performance falls away due to completion of works after the letter of claim. The same principle has been applied in unreported decisions where specific performance had fallen away by virtue of the tenant vacating the property.

For example, in *Gemma Court v Beyond Housing Limited* (12/02/26) HHJ Robinson, sitting in Teeside Combined Court Centre allowed an appeal from a District Judge who did not include provision for costs on the fast-track for legal costs incurred prior to completion of repairs. The Claimant issued proceedings seeking damages of more than £5,000 but less than £10,000 and repairs estimated at more than £1,000. The Claimant relied on an expert report which valued the repairs at £1061.34 plus VAT. The Defendant's expert valued the repairs at just £243.16. At a directions and allocation hearing on 6 November 2024 the claim was allocated to the small claims track on the basis that the repairs had been completed on 30 September 2024. The District Judge determined not to make an order for costs in the case, on the fast-track, in relation to costs incurred prior to the completion of the repair works. The Claimant appealed on three grounds included misdirection/misconstruction of CPR 26.9 and misunderstanding/misapplying binding caselaw, namely *Birmingham v Lee*. HHJ Robinson found that the District Judge erred in her classification of the claim as being and always having been a small claim. HHJ Robinson also noted an absence of reference to *Birmingham v Lee* and, critically, no reason for not following that decision. The small claims track was not the normal track given the pleaded values. The Court was satisfied that the estimated costs of the repairs were in excess of £1,000 based on what the Claimant would need to pay on the open market basis. The Court was also satisfied that the value of the damages would surpass the £1,000 threshold. Having regard to *Birmingham v Lee* and all other factors, including compliance with the pre-action protocol and the overriding objective, the Court varied the order such that the Claimant should be entitled to her costs in the case on the fast track for costs incurred prior to completion of the repairs of the property.

Expert Valuations

In considering allocation, the Court will have regard to the value of the claim and the estimated cost of the repairs.

This was one of the issues considered by District Judge Haisley in the matter of *Jalili v Bury Council* (17/06/21 G00LV579). The Claimant engaged solicitors in October 2017 and then instructed an expert surveyor in November 2017. The Council instructed its own expert surveyor and the respective experts provided a joint report dated 22 February 2018. There was disagreement between the experts as to the precise nature and extent of the works that were necessary. The experts also disagreed in terms of the value of the necessary works- with the Claimant's expert valuing the works at a cost of £3,915 and the Defendant valuing the works at £740. A fundamental difference between the approaches of the two experts was that the Claimant's expert valued the necessary works on an open market basis, whereas the Defendant's expert did not. The Defendant's expert valued the works on the basis that they were to be carried out by the Defendant's in-house team. As it happened, the actual works carried out were those identified by the Defendant's expert, not the more extensive works identified by the Claimant's expert. Those repairs were completed in May 2018. Damages were subsequently agreed in the sum of £1,000 in July 2019. No proceedings had been issued and therefore allocation had not taken place. Costs could not be agreed and therefore Part 8 proceedings were issued to enable the Court to undertake a detailed assessment. The Court acknowledged that when assessing costs on the standard basis, of a claim which concluded without being allocated to a track, it may restrict those costs to costs that would have been allowed on the track to which the claim would have been allocated if allocation had taken place. The Defendant argued that the claim would have been allocated to the small claims track and therefore the Judge should restrict the Claimant to the costs that would have been allowed on the small claims track. To answer this question, the Court has to consider that value of the claim for repairs.

> *"17. It seems to me that the answer to this question lies in the nature of the relief sought. In relation to issue 1 the relief sought was an order for specific performance which I remind myself is an equitable remedy, which is an order requiring the Defendant to perform its part of the bargain, in other words, in this case, to carry out the repairs that it was contractually obliged to under the relevant tenancy agreement.*
>
> *18. That being so, it seems to me that the court cannot and must not close its eyes to the fact that, in essence, the order for specific performance would have required the Defendant, namely Bury Council, to put right the disrepair.*
>
> *19. Consequently, the work would not be ordered to be carried out on the open market; it would be an order requiring a local authority which, as is common knowledge, would have its own in-house team of the relevant professionals undertaking the work, so it seems to me that the Claimant's surveyor's basis of valuing the requisite works was flawed, or certainly was not the relevant basis of valuing the relevant works for the purposes of this issue.*
>
> *20. For the purposes of resolving the question of the value of the claim for specific performance, the open market valuation is not the relevant valuation in my judgment, it is valuation of the work being carried out by the Defendant itself, and so it seems to me that the approach to the question of valuation*

> *taken by the Defendant's surveyor in the joint report is the more appropriate basis.*
>
> *21. Also, the parties appear to have implicitly accepted that the Defendant's surveyor had more accurately identified the nature and extent of the relevant works required to be carried out because it was only those works that had been identified by the Defendant's surveyor which came to be carried out, and those works were carried out to the satisfaction of the Claimant, such that once those works had been completed, there subsisted no longer any claim for specific performance.*
>
> *22. It seems to me, therefore, that the cost of the repairs to the relevant premises was not more than £1,000. In fact, it seems to me, on the balance of probabilities, it was significantly less, and on that basis, on issue 1, were the court looking at the question of to which track this claim would have been allocated by reference solely to the value of repairs, it would have been allocated to the small claims track, and so again for the purposes of issue 1 the court would restrict, applying the overriding objective, the costs payable to costs that would have been allowed on the small claims track, which is the track to which the claim would have been allocated if allocation had taken place for the purposes of 46.13(3)"*

But this is not a binding decision, and there seems to be conflicting first instance decisions. Take for example the Judgment of His Honour Judge Blohm KC in *Stojalowski v Bristol City Council* (11/12/24 L00BS071). This was a decision to determine the appropriate allocation of the claim. The matter originally went before a Deputy District Judge who adjourned the hearing to HHJ Blohm KC for the purpose of providing guidance to local judges faced with the same issues. The Claimant sent a letter of claim and valued the repairs on an open market basis at £1431.68 inclusive of VAT. The

Defendant, on receipt of the letter of claim, initiated its Internal Complaints Procedure (ICP). Following an inspection of the property by Mr Brown, the Defendant produced an ICP Stage 1 decision which partially upheld the complaint of disrepair and offered £833.90 compensation to the Claimant. The Claimant did not initiate Stage 2 of the ICP, and instead issued proceedings on 23 January 2024 alleging that the costs of the repairs exceeded £1,000 and the damages too exceeded £1,000. The Claimant relied upon a report of Mr Lloyd dated 23 September 2023. The Defendant contended that it has complied with its contractual and statutory duties to repair and carry out the works in a reasonably timely manner and with due care and skill. The Defendant relied on the report of Mr Brown. The loss and damages, other than that referred to in the Stage 1 response, was not admitted, save for the £833.90 which had been offered as compensation. On 8 May 2024 the claim was stated for Stage 2 of the ICP to be completed, but ultimately settlement was not reached. The Claimant submitted that the claim was suitable for allocation to the fast-track until such time as the repairs had been fully completed. The Defendant asserted that the sum of £833.90 should be taken into account, and deducted, from the value of damages and that the Court will not grant specific performance against a local authority landlord that was seeking to carry out its contractual obligations. The court considered the two-stage approach of identifying the normal track and then considering CPR 26.13. In considering CPR 26.9, the requirements of CPR 26.9(1)(b) were, on their literal working, made out. The Court did not accept that specific performance was not an available remedy. The Defendant challenged the stated costs of the works on the basis that Mr Lloyd's report was dated, that many of the defects had been cured and that the Defendant would be relying on contracts that were economical. The Defendant argued that the costs of the works to them would likely be less than £1,000. The Court concluded that the costs of the outstanding works on the open market was likely to be more than £1,000. In distinguishing this case from *Jalili*, the Court identified that the Defendant has not adduced its own estimate of costs and there was evidence that the Defendant was using external contractors. Furthermore, in *Jalili* the work had been done. Finally, if necessary, HHJ Blohm took the view that *Jalili* was wrongly decided and that cost should refer to the open market cost of carrying out the works. As for the value of damages, even taking into account the £833.90 which had been admitted/offered, the Judge was satisfied that the value of damages exceeded £1,000. It followed that the normal track for the case would not be the small claims track. In applying the second stage test of considering CPR 26.13, the Judge concluded that the effect of allocation on the housing function of the Defendant was not a matter that should ordinarily have weight in respect of an allocation decision. The Court did have regard to the value of the claim and the likely evidence that would be relied upon and given by the parties. The Judge concluded that the claim should be allocated to the fast track.

In commenting on any failure to engage with the ICP/ADR the Court said:

> *The failure of the claimant to engage with ICP (if this is correct) is not a matter that is pertinent to allocation. If a litigant does not engage with appropriate Alternative Dispute Resolution ('ADR'), then the other party may apply for an appropriate stay for the process to be worked through. That is what happened in this case, and the court directed accordingly. If a party still considers that the process has not been carried out and should be further proceeded with, than a further application may be made. That has not occurred in this case and hence the matter has proceeded to allocation. If a party has wrongly refused to entertain ADR, then that is a matter that the court can and will take into account in determining and assessing costs at the conclusion of the case.*

The council had not adduced its own estimate of costs. The council was using external contracts, so the in-house marginal costs basis would not apply. In Jalili the work had been done. "Cost" here should refer to the local open market costs of carrying out the works.

Exaggeration

Whilst it could be tempting for Claimants to seek to inflate valuations for the purpose of allocation, this could have serious consequences including arguments of abuse of process, contempt of court and costs consequences.

Notably under CPR 44.11 the Court has the power to disallow all or part of the costs being assessed where it appears to the Court that the conduct of a party, before or during the proceedings, was unreasonable or improper.

In *Devine v Franklin* [2002] EWHC 1846 (QB) a successful Claimant who exaggerated his injuries and claim for damages was confined to the fixed costs permitted for a small claims track case. The Claimant was confined to the costs to which he would have been entitled had there been no exaggeration. The Claimant was also entitled to recover a sum in respect of the unreasonable behaviour of the Defendant.

In *Morrow v Shrewsbury Rugby Union Football Club Ltd* [2020] EWHC 999 (QB) (30 April 2020) the Claimant was found to have exaggerated the claim and was deprived of 15% of its costs, despite beating the Defendant's Part 36 offer of £110,000 by a considerable margin, having pleaded a claim in excess of £1 million and recovered damages of £285,658.08.

Summary

In considering allocation, the Court will have regard to the estimated cost of the repairs, the value of the damages claimed and the factors set out at CPR 23.13. Allocation arguments are common in disrepair claims as the recoverable costs on the small claims track are limited. Landlords can mitigate this risk by promptly undertaking repairs.

CHAPTER FOUR

EXPERT EVIDENCE

Expert evidence is often central to disrepair claims. But the notion that each party should obtain its own expert evidence in every case should be carefully considered.

Increasingly, Courts are considering whether expert evidence was required and, if so, whether a single joint expert should have been appointed, and, finally, whether the fees incurred are reasonable and proportionate.

Referring back to the PAP, the Letter of Claim should contain details of the proposed expert and the proposed letter of instruction to the expert (5.2). The Landlord's response should then indicate whether the proposed single joint expert is agreed and whether the letter of instruction is agreed (6.2). If the appointment of a single joint expert is not agreed, then the Landlord should state whether it agrees to a joint inspection.

Section 7 of the PAP deals with Experts. It starts with a reminder that the Civil Procedure Rules provide that expert evidence should be restricted to that which is necessary and that the Court's permission is required to use an expert's report. The Court may limit the amount of experts' fees and expenses recoverable from another party.

Section 7.7 provides that the expert's terms and fees should be agreed at the outset. If there is a single joint expert, then each party will pay half of the costs of the inspection and report. Naturally if each party instructs their own expert, then they are liable for the costs of their own expert's fees.

Bryant v Trivallis and Griffiths v Trivallis (Cardiff County Court, unreported, 3 July 2023)

In this case the HHJ James was considering applications and case management issues in two housing disrepair claims. Whilst these claims were under the Wales protocol, the Court commented that there was no material difference insofar as it concerned the instruction of experts.

In the Bryant case, the Claimant sent a letter of claim on 13 May 2021. The Claimant also proposed a single joint expert. The Defendant sent a response to the letter of claim and attached a schedule of repairs and proposed works. The Defendant objected to obtaining any expert evidence. The Defendant also objected to the proposed expert and nominated an alternative expert. The Defendant attempted to arrange appointments to carry out the repairs, but had been unable to gain access. The Claimant proceeded to instruct an expert that had not been named and without further consultation with the Defendant.

The facts in the Griffiths cases were broadly the same, save that the expert nominated by the Claimant was the surveyor who inspected the property. But, again, the Defendant had objected to the Claimant obtaining expert evidence.

The Court found that there had been a wholesale disregard of the protocol by the Claimants in both cases. Where the Defendant has provided an assessment of the property by a suitably qualified employee, it is incumbent on the Claimant to set out why an expert was still necessary and to respond to the works proposed.

Where the landlord confirms items of disrepair and provides a schedule of work, the necessity of an expert's report can only be assessed once those works are completed.

If an expert is required, it should be a single joint expert unless there are cogent reasons, and the court expects the parties to co-operate in this respect. Separately instructed experts should be very much the exception.

Whilst the Claimants avoided having their claims struck out, they were both refused permission to rely on the expert reports obtained. The Court ordered that there shall be a single joint expert instead.

Lancastle v Curo Group (Albion) Limited (Bristol County Court 23/06/25)

In this case, HHJ Blohm KC was also considering two housing disrepair claims (Lancastle & Bailey). The Defendants applied to have the claims struck out, alternative summary judgment in their favour and in the further alternative a directions debarring the Claimants from relying on their chosen expert evidence.

In Bailey, the Claimants sent a letter of claim and provided the CV of ten surveyors from C7 surveyors for consideration as a single joint expert. However they failed to provide any costs for the work, basis of charging, or rates. The Defendant wished to inspect the property and challenged the need for expert evidence. The Defendant also objected to the proposed surveyors on the basis that they were not local and that no fee has been provided. Following the Defendant's inspection the Claimant proceeded to obtain expert evidence.

In Lancastle, the facts were broadly the same. The Defendant opposed the instruction of an expert until the complaints process was completed and asserted that, if an expert was needed, it should be a single joint expert. The Claimant proceeded to instruct an expert, before the agreed date for the Defendant's response to the letter of claim.

In neither case had the letter of claim set out the fees of the surveyor and in each case the surveyors proposed by the Claimants were not local. The Court found that there was good reasons for not agreeing to, or objecting to, the proposed surveyors.

The case of *Bryant v Trevillis* was relied upon by the Defendants.

The Court found that there was an obligation on Claimants to engage with a Defendant's response before obtaining expert evidence. In considering the appropriateness of instructing an expert, the Court approached the issue in the following way:

> *(1) The reliance by Curo on Protocol 7.1(a) is misplaced. This is a warning to the parties that in litigation the court will only allow expert evidence to be adduced (and therefore potentially fall within a costs entitlement one way or the other) if it considers that it is reasonably required to resolve the proceedings (CPR 35.1). It is not a prohibition on adducing expert evidence at this stage in accordance with the Protocol.*
>
> *(2) It goes almost without saying that parties should only adduce expert evidence where there is a dispute. If the initial response concedes the defects alleged and the work required, then the only outstanding issue is likely to be the level of damages, and expert evidence is unlikely to be necessary to resolve that. (3) Specific performance may be in dispute even if the defects are not. Although the lessor may select the means of remedying the defect where there is more than one, that means must be reasonable – see Dame Margaret Hungerford v Beazeley [1994] 26 HLR 269, and there may be a dispute as to whether the selected means is reasonable.*

(4) The appointment of an expert must be done in good faith; that is, for the genuine purpose of resolving a dispute between the parties.

(5) The Protocol is based on the presumption that at this stage, whether or not the landlord has provided a reasoned letter of response, expert evidence will usually be required, and that evidence should be a Single Joint Expert, but if not then will probably be one of two experts who will examine at the same time by a joint inspection.

(6) It is open to a landlord to object to the identity of the expert put forward by the tenant – see Protocol para 7.2(a)). In many cases the landlord will know nothing about the expert and will have to rely on his CV and his qualifications and consequential independence and objectivity. That is inherent in the Protocol and CPR Part 35. If he does object for an arguable reason, then the parties must seek to negotiate an acceptable SJE. They must act reasonably in so doing (Bryant v Trevallis). I consider it unlikely that the fact that a surveyor s habitually instructed by tenants, or is on a tenant's panel, would be an arguable ground for disqualification. Any professional will be subject to the obligations of his profession, and the requirements of CPR 35 are clear.

(7) The Protocol does not require the obtaining of expert's evidence to be deferred simply because a Letter of Response has been obtained. The general tenor of the Protocol is that this should be a speedy process, because the tenant may well be enduring very unpleasant living conditions. However, if the tenant does not consider the Letter of Response and engage with it (in the very broad sense I have outlined above – by telling the landlord that the matter is in dispute) then a court

may consider subsequently that the appointment of an expert has not been made in good faith.

(8) That the landlord has had the building examined by an expert does not in my view alter matters. If the landlord is in the fortunate position of being able to rely on in-house expertise, then that is its benefit. To the extent that it admits defects, and proposes remedies, then the tenant may be more inclined to accept those proposals as reasonable remediation. But if it denies the defects or proposes a limited basis for the remedial works, then the tenant can I consider reasonably say that the time has come for the expert contemplated by the Protocol to be appointed.

(9) It will normally be difficult for a court to find that an expert has been appointed in bad faith at this stage of proceedings.

(10) The 'Take Stock' direction at paragraph 8 of the Protocol provides:

> *"Taking stock*
>
> *8 Where the procedure set out in this Protocol has not resolved the dispute between the landlord and the tenant, they should undertake a review of their respective positions to see if proceedings can be avoided and, at the least, to narrow the issues between them."*

This does not mean that the parties must take stock of their respective positions before instructing experts; it requires them to take stock at the conclusion of the Protocol's process, and before issuing proceedings.

The Court concluded that there had been a failure on the part of the Claimants to comply with the pre-action protocol by failing to provide the fees or charging rates of the proposed experts, instructing the experts prematurely, failing to engage with the Defendant on the issue of expert evidence and failing to provide the expert with the response from the Defendant.

These breaches did not justify striking out the claim or barring the expert reports. Instead the Court considered that an appropriate order should be that the Claimants be precluded from recovering the costs of instructing and obtaining the evidence of their respective experts, whatever the outcome of the litigation. Furthermore, if the Defendant wished to raise Part 35 questions of the experts in respect of matters contained within their letters of responses, the cost of that process would also be borne by the Claimants in each case.

The Court then helpfully summarised the points of principle that had been expressed:

> *(1) It is open to a tenant to extend the initial period of 20 days for the landlord to respond under the Protocol, by agreement;*
>
> *(2) If the tenant so agrees, the period within the Protocol for instructing an expert is consequently extended;*
>
> *(3) A tenant is under an obligation to consider a landlord's response if given in this initial period prior to instructing an expert under the Protocol;*
>
> *(4) Exactly what a tenant's further response should be depends on the facts of the case, but at the least the tenant should notify the landlord that the landlord's response is not accepted and (if it be the case) that the tenant is proceeding to instruct an expert;*

> *(5) The decision on the part of the tenant to instruct an expert at this stage is contemplated by the Protocol; it is unlikely to be susceptible to challenge unless made in bad faith;*
>
> *(6) The landlord should be supplied with the charging rate or costs of the proposed expert prior to his being instructed;*
>
> *(7) If the expert is instructed as a sole expert he should be supplied with the landlord's letter of response;*
>
> *(8) A failure to comply with paras (3), (6) and (7) above may well give rise to sanctions preventing the tenant from recovering the costs of his expert from the landlord;*
>
> *(9) The mere fact that a landlord has obtained an in-house report from a qualified person does not necessarily mean that the landlord will be precluded by the court from obtaining or relying on an expert's report, whether it is the same inhouse report in a form compliant with CPR 35 or some other expert.*

The fees charged by experts can differ quite significantly. If a paying party wishes to challenge the fee of an expert, it would be prudent to make evidence-based objections i.e. providing evidence that experts providing similar reports charge less.

Summary

Careful consideration should be given as to the need for expert evidence. Where expert evidence is required, this should usually be on a single joint basis.

CHAPTER FIVE

PROPORTIONALITY

General principles

Costs play a significant role in housing disrepair claims for several reasons.

Firstly, damages are often low to moderate. Many claims settle for less than £10,000, however the Claimant's costs can easily exceed those figures, and often do. It would not be uncommon to see a claim settle for around £1,000 in damages where costs are claimed at over £10,000.

Secondly, many claims are brought with the benefit of a CFA. In practice this means the Claimant has little incentive to control its own costs. However, costs recovery becomes essential to the economic sustainability of those firms bringing such claims. Therefore, it is the Claimant law firms which typically have the greatest interest in maximising the amount of costs recovered. By contrast, if a Claimant was privately funding the litigation using their own resources, you would have to question whether they would be willing to incur £10,000 in costs to only recover £1,000 in damages.

Thirdly, landlords- particularly public bodies- are acutely sensitive to legal spend. The costs arising from such claims are ultimately funded by public money.

Damages are often awarded or agreed in respect of general damages for inconvenience and loss of amenity, special damages for damages to belongings and sometimes damages for personal injury. Often the level of damages is abated to account for rent arrears. But proportionality is not simply assessing the value of the claim against the costs. Most claims seek specific performance- i.e. fixing the disrepair. Claimants will often argue that this weighs more heavily than financial compensation.

CPR 44.3(2) provides that where costs are payable on the standard basis, the Court will only allow costs which are proportionate to the matters in issue. Costs which are disproportionate may be disallowed or reduced even if they were reasonable and necessary. The rule goes on to say that any doubt as to whether costs are reasonable or proportionate will be resolved in favour of the paying party.

CPR 44.3 (5) provides that:

> *(5) Costs incurred are proportionate if they bear a reasonable relationship to –*
>
> > *(a) the sums in issue in the proceedings;*
> >
> > *(b) the value of any non-monetary relief in issue in the proceedings;*
> >
> > *(c) the complexity of the litigation;*
> >
> > *(d) any additional work generated by the conduct of the paying party,*
> >
> > *(e) any wider factors involved in the proceedings, such as reputation or public importance; and*
> >
> > *(f) any additional work undertaken or expense incurred due to the vulnerability of a party or any witness.*

In the context of housing disrepair claims, the sums in issue are relatively easy to identify. The non-monetary relief will typically be the claim for specific performance. Complexity is subjective with paying parties often submitting that such claims are not complex, but receiving parties contending that they are.

Conduct often plays a significant role in considering proportionality. If a paying party's conduct has caused an increase in costs, then this will be taken into account when assessing proportionality. By contrast if the receiving party's own conduct has caused an increase in costs, then this may weigh against them. The Court will of course have regard to the party's compliance with the Pre-Action Protocol.

Reputation or public importance tend to weigh less heavily. That said, examples of disrepair which have led to medical conditions have been a matter of public importance and have led to changes in the law. For example, *Awaab's Law* was introduced on 27 October 2025 and was named after two-year-old Awaab Ishak who died in December 2020 due to respiratory condition caused by prolonged exposure to mold. This new law imposes a requirement upon landlords to address all emergency hazards and all damp and mould hazards that present a significant risk of harm to tenants to fixed timeframes. The regulations mean landlords must:

- Investigate any potential emergency hazards and, if the investigation confirms emergency hazards, undertake relevant safety work as soon as reasonably practicable. The investigation and the work must both take place within 24 hours of becoming aware of the hazard.

- Investigate any potential significant hazards within 10 working days of becoming aware of them.

- Produce a written summary of investigation findings and provide this to the tenant within 3 working days of the conclusion of the investigation.

- Undertake relevant safety work within 5 working days of the investigation concluding, if the investigation identifies a significant hazard.

- Begin, or take steps to begin, any supplementary preventative work to prevent a significant or emergency hazard recurring within 5 working days of the investigation concluding, if the investigation identifies a significant or emergency hazard. If steps cannot be taken to begin work in 5 working days this must be done as soon as possible, and work must be physically started within 12 weeks.

- Satisfactorily complete supplementary preventative works within a reasonable time period.

- Secure the provision of suitable alternative accommodation for the household, at the social landlord's expense, if relevant safety work cannot be completed within specified timeframes.

- Keep the tenant updated throughout the process and provide information on how to keep safe.

If costs have been increased due to the vulnerability of a party or witness, then this will be taken into account. The onus is of course upon the receiving party to demonstrate that the party or witness was vulnerable and how this increased costs. Vulnerability could be because of a personal characteristic such as a health condition or a situation such as a bereavement or homelessness.

Practice Direction 1A provides that:

> *4. Factors which may cause vulnerability in a party or witness include (but are not limited to)—*
>
> *(a) Age, immaturity or lack of understanding;*

(b) Communication or language difficulties (including literacy);

(c) Physical disability or impairment, or health condition;

(d) Mental health condition or significant impairment of any aspect of their intelligence or social functioning (including learning difficulties);

(e) The impact on them of the subject matter of, or facts relevant to, the case (an example being having witnessed a traumatic event relating to the case);

(f) Their relationship with a party or witness (examples being sexual assault, domestic abuse or intimidation (actual or perceived));

(g) Social, domestic or cultural circumstances.

Case Law

Mr Justice Legatt was considering an application for a payment on account of costs in *Kazakhstan Kagazy plc v Zhunus* [2015] EWHC 404 (Comm). At paragraph 13 he said:

> *"13. In a case such as this where very large amounts of money are at stake, it may be entirely reasonable from the point of view of a party incurring costs to spare no expense that might possibly help to influence the result of the proceedings. It does not follow, however, that such expense should be regarded as reasonably or proportionately incurred or reasonable and proportionate in amount when it comes to determining what costs are recoverable from the other party. What is reasonable and proportionate in that context must be judged objectively.*

> *The touchstone is not the amount of costs which it was in a party's best interests to incur but the lowest amount which it could reasonably have been expected to spend in order to have its case conducted and presented proficiently, having regard to all the relevant circumstances. Expenditure over and above this level should be for a party's own account and not recoverable from the other party. This approach is first of all fair. It is fair to distinguish between, on the one hand, costs which are reasonably attributable to the other party's conduct in bringing or contesting the proceeding or otherwise causing costs to be incurred and, on the other hand, costs which are attributable to a party's own choice about how best to advance its interests. There are also good policy reasons for drawing this distinction, which include discouraging waste and seeking to deter the escalation of costs for the overall benefit for litigants.".*

As against the costs of around £945,000, Mr Justice Legatt ordered £220,000 should be paid by way of interim payment. He reached this conclusion by first estimating that the sum likely to be recoverable would be in the region of £325,000, against which an interim payment of £220,000 would be reasonable. This methodology for determining an appropriate level of an interim payment is not controversial and reflects *Mars UK Ltd v Teknowledge Ltd* [1999] and has been applied more recently in *Mousavi-Khalkali v Abrishamchi & Anor* [2020] EWCA Civ 1493 (12 November 2020).

However, the comments made as to proportionality were more controversial. Neither the CPR or leading authorities supported the notion that a proportionate amount is the lowest amount that could reasonably have been incurred.

Mr Eggers KC in *Discovery Land Company, LLC & Ors v Axis Specialty Europe SE* [2021] EWHC 2146 (Comm) (30 July 2021), addressed this as follows:

> *"Of course, costs must be assessed in the manner that Leggatt, J indicated in this judgment. I have only one reservation. I am not certain why the "touchstone" of reasonable or proportionate costs must be the lowest amount which a party could reasonably have been expected to spend. Certainly in the context of costs management, the Court should allow some flexibility to the parties to ensure that their conduct of the action is not unnecessarily and potentially unfairly hampered by an unrealistically low assessment or by only the lowest assessment of what would constitute reasonable and proportionate expenditure. Expenditure which is within a reasonable and proportionate range is still reasonable and proportionate even if it is not at the lower end.".*

Mr Eggers KC was considering proportionality in the context of costs management.

Lead Authority

In 2019 practitioners received what is now the lead authority on proportionality in *West v Stockport NHS Foundation Trust* [2019] EWCA Civ 1220 (17 July 2019). This effectively replaced the "Lownds test" from *Lownds v Home Office* [2002]. This decision by the Court of Appeal was primarily an appeal arising from the amount of an ATE premium. However, the Court of Appeal also took the opportunity to lay out a new test for proportionality.

> *87. We are anxious not to restrict judges or force them, when assessing a bill of costs, to follow inflexible or overly-complex*

rules. One of the matters, however, which is apparent from the many cases cited to us, and from the submissions of counsel on the hearing of these appeals, is that there is an absence of consistency in the way in which costs bills are assessed. <u>Taking the various points made above and drawing them together, we give the following guidance on an appropriate approach</u>.

88. *<u>First, the judge should go through the bill line-by-line, assessing the reasonableness of each item of cost. If the judge considers it possible, appropriate and convenient when undertaking that exercise, he or she may also address the proportionality of any particular item at the same time</u>. That is because, although reasonableness and proportionality are conceptually distinct, there can be an overlap between them, not least because reasonableness may be a necessary condition of proportionality: see Rogers at paragraph 104. This will be a matter for the judge. It will apply, for example, when the judge considers an item to be clearly disproportionate, irrespective of the final figures.*

89. *At the conclusion of the line-by-line exercise, there will be a total figure which the judge considers to be reasonable (and which may, as indicated, also take into account at least some aspects of proportionality). That total figure will have involved an assessment of every item of cost, including court fees, the ATE premium and the like.*

90. *The proportionality of that total figure must be assessed by reference to both r.44.3(5) and r.44.4(1). If that total figure is found to be proportionate, then no further assessment is required<u>. If the judge regards the overall figure as disproportionate, then a further assessment is required. That should not be line-by-line, but should instead consider</u>*

various categories of cost, such as disclosure or expert's reports, or specific periods where particular costs were incurred, or particular parts of the profit costs.

91. *At that stage, however, any reductions for proportionality should exclude those elements of costs which are properly regarded as unavoidable, such as court fees, the reasonable element of the ATE premium in clinical negligence cases, and the like. Specifically, therefore, if the ATE premium is assessed as reasonable, it will not fall to be reduced by any further assessment of proportionality.*

92. *The judge will undertake the proportionality assessment by looking at the different categories of costs (excluding the unavoidable items noted above) and considering, in respect of each such category, whether the costs incurred were disproportionate. If yes, then the judge will make such reduction as is appropriate. In that way, reductions for proportionality will be clear and transparent for both sides.*

93. *Once any further reductions have been made, the resulting figure will be the final amount of the costs assessment. There would be no further stage of standing back and, if necessary, undertaking a yet further review by reference to proportionality. That would introduce the risk of double-counting.*

Commonly referred to as the *West Test*, this is lead authority on how the Court should approach proportionality when assessing costs on the standard basis.

Summary

Proportionality is a subjective test which is at the discretion of the Judge having regard to all the factors at CPR 44.3(5). Costs which are disproportionate may be disallowed or reduced even if they were reasonable and necessary.

CHAPTER SIX

HOURLY RATES

Application of Guideline Hourly Rates

> *"...If a rate in excess of the guideline rate is to be charged to the paying party, a clear and compelling justification must be provided. It is not enough to say that the case is a commercial case, or a competition case, or that it has an international element, unless there is something about these factors in the case in question which justifies exceeding the guideline rate."*

This part of the Judgment from Lord Justice Males in *Samsung Electronics Co. Ltd & Ors v LG Display Co. Ltd & Anor* (Costs) [2022] EWCA Civ 466 (06 April 2022) is perhaps the most quoted judgment by paying parties who seek to limit hourly rates to the guidelines. It has certainly gained traction in the High Courts (see *Athena Capital Fund SICAV-FIS SCA v Secretariat of State for the Holy See* (Costs) [2022] EWCA Civ 1061, *Manek & Ors v 360 One WAM Ltd & Ors* (Re Consequentials) [2023] EWHC 985 (Comm) (28 April 2023) and *Otto & Ors v Inner Mongolia Happy Lamb Catering Management Company Ltd & Ors* [2023] EWHC 3151 (Ch) (08 December 2023)).

However, this is not so readily accepted by Costs Judges who conduct detailed assessment. The current Senior Costs Judge, Costs Judge Rowley, addressed this in his judgment in *Various Claimants v News Group Newspapers Ltd* [2023] EWHC 827 (SCCO) (04 April 2023). He says:

> *"I also accept the argument that the GHR may be a useful starting point in a detailed assessment as well as in a summary assessment. I do not, however, consider that the guidance*

> *given by Males LJ regarding the need for a "clear and compelling justification" for exceeding the GHR extends with any great force to this particular situation.*

The GHR are provided predominantly to assist judges who do not specialise in costs cases to deal with a summary assessment of costs when faced with the successful party's summary assessment schedule and competing arguments from the advocates.

The relevance to the GHR being a starting point in detailed assessments is no more than a reflection of the scarcity of any other starting point. Expense of time calculations or other potential starting points, as is demonstrated here, are invariably absent. But a starting point by its very name does not suggest it is the finishing point and that is particularly so where the court has the opportunity for the parties to address it in detail in respect of the CPR 44.4 factors."

The CPR 44.4(3) factors

CPR 44.4(3) provides that when assessing costs the Court will have regard to:

> *(a) the conduct of all the parties, including in particular –*
>
> > *(i) conduct before, as well as during, the proceedings; and*
> >
> > *(ii) the efforts made, if any, before and during the proceedings in order to try to resolve the dispute;*
>
> *(b) the amount or value of any money or property involved;*
>
> *(c) the importance of the matter to all the parties;*

(d) the particular complexity of the matter or the difficulty or novelty of the questions raised;

(e) the skill, effort, specialised knowledge and responsibility involved;

(f) the time spent on the case;

(g) the place where and the circumstances in which work or any part of it was done; and

(h) the receiving party's last approved or agreed budget.

Effectively this means that in deciding whether the rate agreed between the Claimant and their solicitor was reasonable, the Court will have regard to some factors which unfold during the course of the claim. A solicitor will perhaps have a feel for the value of the claim and the complexity of the matter at the outset, but issues such as conduct only arise once the claim is afoot.

It follows that Defendants wishing to mitigate their liability for costs, by taking steps to reduce the hourly rate which may be recoverable, should ensure they take steps to resolve the claim as efficiently as possible and ensuring their conduct is to the highest standard. This takes the Defendants right back to the PAP. Non-compliance with the PAP by a Defendant will almost certainly be considered when looking at the conduct of the parties and the time spent on the case.

Summary

Assessing hourly rates is a subjective test which is at the discretion of the Judge having regard to all the factors at CPR 44.4(3). It is often difficult to predict with any certainty what rates will be allowed. But for many fast-track disrepair claims, Claimants may struggle to recover much more than the Guideline Hourly Rates.

CHAPTER SEVEN

CONDUCT & MISCONDUCT

The conduct of the parties will be considered whenever the Court is exercising its discretion as to costs (CPR 44.2) and when assessing costs (CPR 44.4). Exemplary conduct by a receiving party or poor conduct by a paying party will often result in a higher award of costs.

However the Court has wider powers where it established that there has been misconduct. The Court's powers in relation to misconduct can be found at CPR 44.11:

> *(1) The court may make an order under this rule where –*
>
> > *(a) a party or that party's legal representative, in connection with a summary or detailed assessment, fails to comply with a rule, practice direction or court order; or*
> >
> > *(b) it appears to the court that the conduct of a party or that party's legal representative, before or during the proceedings or in the assessment proceedings, was unreasonable or improper.*
>
> *(2) Where paragraph (1) applies, the court may –*
>
> > *(a) disallow all or part of the costs which are being assessed; or*
> >
> > *(b) order the party at fault or that party's legal representative to pay costs which that party or legal representative has caused any other party to incur.*

When a receiving party's solicitor signs a bill of costs, they are certifying that the bill is accurate. This is no empty formality (as per *Bailey v IBC Vehicles Ltd* [1998] 2 All ER 570).

Gempride Ltd v Bamrah & Anor [2018] EWCA Civ 1367 is a key Court of Appeal decision establishing that solicitors are responsible for costs-related misconduct by agents (such as cost lawyers) and can face severe penalties under CPR 44.11 for certifying inflated or incorrect bills. Ms Bamrah had certified a bill of costs which included hourly rates substantially in excess of that which she was liable to pay and had given an answer to a point of dispute that was untrue or misleading. The Court of Appeal, in allowing the appeal, ordered a 50% reduction to be applied to the assessed costs.

The Court of Appeal, at paragraph 26, neatly summarised this position as follows:

> *i) A solicitor as a legal representative owes a duty to the court, and remains responsible for the conduct of anyone to whom he subcontracts work that he (the solicitor) is retained to do. That is particularly so where the subcontractor is not a legal representative and so does not himself owe an independent duty to the court.*
>
> *ii) Whilst "unreasonable" and "improper" conduct are not self-contained concepts, "unreasonable" is essentially conduct which permits of no reasonable explanation, whilst "improper" has the hallmark of conduct which the consensus of professional opinion would regard as improper.*
>
> *iii) Mistake or error of judgment or negligence, without more, will be insufficient to amount to "unreasonable or improper" conduct.*

> *iv) Although the conduct of the relevant legal representative must amount to a breach of duty owed by the representative to the court to perform his duty to the court, the conduct does not have be in breach of any formal professional rule nor dishonest.*
>
> *v) Where an application under CPR rule 44.11 is made, the burden of proof lies on the applicant in the sense that the court cannot make an order unless it is satisfied that the conduct was "unreasonable or improper".*
>
> *vi) Even where the threshold criteria are satisfied, the court still has a discretion as to whether to make an order.*
>
> *vii) If the court determines to make an order, any order made (or "sanction") must be proportionate to the misconduct as found, in all the circumstances.*

In *Farmer v The Chief Constable of Lancashire* [2019] EWHC B18 (Costs) (31 October 2019), the bill started at £174,565.79. One of the CFAs was found to be unenforceable, and the second CFA did not have the retrospective effect that the Claimant contended for. There were further issues, such as the incorrect rates being claimed. The Court found that the bill, properly drawn, should have been in the region of £66,773.10. The Court's decision is summarised from paragraphs 34:

> *34. Therefore, where we are now is we have a bill of £59,933.10 – or 34% of the bill as originally lodged – and numerous examples of documents, specifically the bill, the replies and the witness statement, which have been signed without any proper regard for the need to fact-check and ensure that matters were dealt with properly.*

> *35. I agree with Mr Smith, as well as being unreasonable or improper – which Mr Edwards accepts that it was – the conduct of McMillan Williams up to and including the witness statement of the costs lawyer has been in breach of the Civil Procedure Rules, and especially of the provisions of CPR 1.3 whereby the parties are required to help the Court to further the overriding objective.*
>
> *36. I was grateful to Mr Edwards for his learned submissions on the law, but again I am not going to go through it in any detail. I am, of course, familiar with Bamrah and, in particular, MXX as I was an assessor in that case.*
>
> *37. This case turns on its own facts. In my view, on the facts of this case, the conduct of McMillan Williams (as set out above) warrants disallowance of what is left of the bill. That is what I order.*

Due to unreasonable or improper conduct, as well as the non-compliance with the CPR, the Court concluded that it was just to disallow the entirety of the Claimant's costs.

In *Hyder v Aidat-Sarran & Anor* [2024] EWHC 3686 (SCCO) (09 December 2024) the Court was satisfied that there had been misconduct in the detailed assessment proceedings and imposed a 75% reduction to be applied to the assessed costs.

Examples of common allegations of misconduct which arise in HDR claims:

- Non-compliance with the PAP;
- Premature issuance of proceedings;

- Refusing access to undertake repairs;
- Use of an expert firm or expert agency where there is a potential conflict (i.e. the law firm has an interest in the expert firm);
- Misstating the qualification or grade of the fee earner; and
- Pro-forma time recording.

Whether these amount to misconduct is a matter for the discretion of the Court, but each would give rise to considering the question of conduct.

Summary

Whilst conduct is a matter which will be considered when assessing costs, misconduct can give rise to further costs reductions.

CHAPTER EIGHT

STANDARD V INDEMNITY BASIS

Whether the costs are assessed on the standard or indemnity basis, they must be reasonably incurred and reasonable in amount.

Where the costs are to be assessed on the standard basis, the Court will only allow costs which are proportionate to the matters in issue. Costs which are disproportionate in amount may be disallowed or reduced even if they were reasonably or necessarily incurred.

On the standard basis, the Court will resolve any doubt which it may have as to whether costs were reasonably and proportionately incurred or were reasonable and proportionate in amount in favour of the paying party.

Where the amount of costs is to be assessed on the indemnity basis, the Court will resolve any doubt which it may have as to whether costs were reasonably incurred or were reasonable in amount in favour of the receiving party.

Statement	Standard Basis	Indemnity Basis
Costs must be reasonably incurred and reasonable in amount.	Yes	Yes
Costs must be proportionate.	Yes	No
Doubt resolved in favour of the paying party.	Yes	No
Court will have regard to the last approved budget	Yes	No
Court will not depart from the last agreed or approved budget unless there is good reason.	Yes	No

There are various rules of thumb which are often discussed, such as that a party might recover 60-80% on the standard basis whereas it is more likely to recover 80-90% on the indemnity basis. Whilst this may often be the case, it is just as often that it is not the case, making this rule of thumb quite unreliable. Fundamentally the amount recovered is specific to each case.

Summary

Whether the costs are to be assessed on the standard or indemnity basis, the costs must still be reasonably incurred and reasonable in amount. Whilst a party can generally expect to recover more on the indemnity basis, there is no reliable rule of thumb. Detailed assessments are often won and lost on the quality of the file. Well organised files, with well documented attendance notes, are likely to result in a better outcome at detailed assessment.

CHAPTER NINE

ASSESSMENTS OF COSTS

Timetable

The procedure for assessment of costs is provided at CPR 47.

Step	When
Commencement of Costs Proceedings- CPR 47.6	Within three months of the authority for costs- CPR 47.7
Service of points of dispute- CPR 47.9	21 days after the date of service of the notice of commencement
Optional reply to points of dispute- CPR 47.13	Within 21 days after being served with the points of dispute
Requesting a detailed assessment hearing- CPR 47.14	Within 3 months of the expiry of the period for commencing detailed assessment proceedings i.e. 6 months from the authority for costs.

Detailed assessment hearing where costs are over £75,000- CPR 47.14 Provisional assessment where costs are under £75,000- CPR 47.15	By direction of the Court once a request has been filed.

General principles

The Court has a wide discretion to exercise when assessing costs. CPR 44.4(3) provides that the Court will have regard to:

> *(a) the conduct of all the parties, including in particular –*
>
> > *(i) conduct before, as well as during, the proceedings; and*
> >
> > *(ii) the efforts made, if any, before and during the proceedings in order to try to resolve the dispute;*
>
> *(b) the amount or value of any money or property involved;*
>
> *(c) the importance of the matter to all the parties;*
>
> *(d) the particular complexity of the matter or the difficulty or novelty of the questions raised;*
>
> *(e) the skill, effort, specialised knowledge and responsibility involved;*
>
> *(f) the time spent on the case;*

> *(g) the place where and the circumstances in which work or any part of it was done; and*
>
> *(h) the receiving party's last approved or agreed budget.*

This is not too dissimilar to the test at CPR 44.3(5) in relation to proportionality.

There is very little guidance in the CPR as to any specific categories of costs which are unreasonable or irrecoverable. The only guidance can be found in Practice Direction 47 which provides that:

> *5.19 The bill of costs must not contain any claims in respect of costs or court fees which relate solely to the detailed assessment proceedings other than costs claimed for preparing and checking the bill.*
>
> ...
>
> *5.22 The following provisions relate to work done by legal representatives —*
>
> > *(1) Routine letters out, routine e-mails out and routine telephone calls will in general be allowed on a unit basis of 6 minutes each, the charge being calculated by reference to the appropriate hourly rate. The unit charge for letters out and e-mails out will include perusing and considering the routine letters in or e-mails in.*
> >
> > *(2) The court may, in its discretion, allow an actual time charge for preparation of electronic communications sent by legal representatives, which properly amount to attendances provided that the time taken has been recorded.*

(3) Local travelling expenses incurred by legal representatives will not be allowed. The definition of 'local' is a matter for the discretion of the court. As a matter of guidance, 'local' will, in general, be taken to mean within a radius of 10 miles from the court dealing with the case at the relevant time. Where travelling and waiting time is claimed, this should be allowed at the rate agreed with the client unless this is more than the hourly rate on the assessment.

(4) The cost of postage, couriers, out-going telephone calls, fax and telex messages will in general not be allowed but the court may exceptionally in its discretion allow such expenses in unusual circumstances or where the cost is unusually heavy.

(5) The cost of making copies of documents will not in general be allowed but the court may exceptionally in its discretion make an allowance for copying in unusual circumstances or where the documents copied are unusually numerous in relation to the nature of the case. Where this discretion is invoked the number of copies made, their purpose and the costs claimed for them must be set out in the bill.

(6) Agency charges as between principal legal representatives and their agents will be dealt with on the principle that such charges, where appropriate, form part of the principal legal representative's charges. Where these charges relate to head (1) in paragraph 5.12 (attendances at court and on counsel) they must be included in their chronological order in that head. In other cases they must be included in head (9) (attendances on London and other agents).

As to the amount of time the Court will allow for specific tasks or disbursements, this is ultimately at the discretion of the Judge.

There are some principles that can be ascertained from case law:

- Inter-fee earner discussions are properly allowable in principle (subject to reasonableness)- *Fuseon Ltd, R (On the Application Of) v Shinners* [2020] EWHC B18 (Costs) (09 April 2020).

- More than one fee earner attending a meeting or Court will rarely be reasonable- *Fuseon Ltd, R (On the Application Of) v Shinners* [2020] EWHC B18 (Costs) (09 April 2020).

- Funding costs (such as drafting retainers) are not generally recoverable- see *Motto & Ors v Trafigura Ltd & Anor (Rev 3)* [2011] EWCA Civ 1150 (12 October 2011).

- Invoicing and credit control is not recoverable- see *Breyer Group & Ors v Prospect Law Limited* (SCCO) (26 July 2017)

Detailed assessments are notoriously unpredictable as the Court has a very wide range of discretion. Where the costs are over £75,000, detailed assessments enable the parties to make oral representations in relation to the costs issues which arise. Whilst this is beneficial in assisting the Court, it can be a costly and time-consuming exercise.

In *Deutsche Bank AG v Sebastian Holdings Inc* [2023] EWHC 9 (SCCO) (23 December 2022) the detailed assessment took around 97 days including preliminary issues hearings. This was more than twice as long as the 44-day trial. The bill of costs was c£62m for which the Defendant was ordered to pay 85% on the indemnity basis. Of the c£53m payable, the Court assessed the costs at c£36m.

Detailed assessments are often won and lost on the quality of the file. Well organised files, with well documented attendance notes, are likely to result in a better outcome at detailed assessment.

Provisional Assessments

Provisional Assessments are conducted where the value of the costs being assessed are under £75,000. This will capture the vast majority of disrepair cases. Generally speaking, the Court might set aside an hour to conduct the exercise. Bills of costs can often be lengthy documents with extensive schedules. Points of dispute are meant to be short and to the point (Practice Direction 47 paragraph 8.2) and replies to points of dispute are optional but should be limited to points of principle and concessions. But often points of dispute will expand across multiple pages, with the replies matching the density of the objections.

This begs the question, under a provisional assessment regime, of how a paying party can fully articulate complex costs arguments, how a receiving party can fully defend its claim for costs and how a Judge conducting an assessment on paper is meant to grapple with these issues without assistance from advocates. Some Courts do not even obtain the receiving party's files and therefore navigating some of the factual issues that can arise must be incredibly difficult. The result is that the Court will do the best it can with what it has.

There is scope for parties to challenge the provisional assessment by way of requesting an oral hearing. Any party which has requested an oral hearing will pay the costs of and incidental to that hearing unless it achieves an adjustment in its own favour by 20% or more of the sum provisionally assessed (unless the Court otherwise orders). It follows that oral hearings are not particularly common as a 20% adjustment is a high hurdle.

Summary

Detailed assessments are notoriously unpredictable. There is no reliable rule of thumb. The merits of an assessment will turn on the factors set out at CPR 44.4(3) and the quality of the time records.

CONCLUSION

Housing Disrepair claims create fertile ground for costs disputes due to the fact that the damages are often relatively modest, the costs often exceed the value of the claim, and many Defendants are seeking to control public funds/expenditure.

Whilst the value of the claim for damages and repairs is a factor, conduct is equally important. A well-conducted claim, or a poorly conducted defence, is likely to result in an increased costs recovery. A poorly conducted claim, or a well conducted defence, is likely to result in a reduced costs recovery.

The importance of the claim for the Claimant is also a key factor that the Court will consider. The fact that a Claimant may be living in an environment which at the very least may be unpleasant, but at worst could be unsafe, will not go unnoticed.

I suspect that such claims will eventually fall under the remit of a Fixed Recoverable Costs regime which may encourage greater co-operation, promote swifter access to justice for Claimants/Tenants and provide greater transparency for Defendants/Landlords. In the meantime, the cost battles in disrepair claims will continue.

MORE BOOKS BY LAW BRIEF PUBLISHING

A selection of our other titles available now:-

'A Practical Guide to Probation Breaches and Other Applications' by Mark Thomas

'A Practical Guide to Remarriage and Divorce' by Cordelia Williams & Claire Howard

'A Practical Guide to Privacy, Transparency, Reporting Restrictions and Closed Proceedings in the Court of Protection' by Laura Mannering

'Beaumont on Barristers – A Guide to Defending Disciplinary Proceedings (Second Edition)' by Marc Beaumont

'A Practical Guide to Payments for Environmental Services' by Ben Sharples

'A Practical Guide to the Law of Pregnancy and Maternity at Work' by Rebecca Thomas

'A Practical Guide to Redundancy – Second Edition' by Philip Hyland & Collette Moore

'A Practical Guide to International Issues for Scottish Family Lawyers' by Susie Mountain, Donna McKay, Ken MacDonald

'A Practical Guide to the Law on Deprivation of Liberty' by Ben Troke

'A Practical Guide to Rights over Airspace and Subsoil – Second Edition' by Daniel Gatty

'A Practical Guide to the Law in Relation to Inquests' by Ramya Nagesh

'A Practical Guide to the Construction and Rectification of Wills and Trust Instruments (Second Edition)' by Edward Hewitt

'A Practical Guide to Data Protection in Social Housing' by Clare Paterson

'A Practical Guide to Spousal Maintenance – Second Edition' by Liz Cowell

'A Practical Guide to International Parental Child Abduction Law (England and Wales)' by Dr Onyója Momoh

'A Practical Guide to Deprivation of British Citizenship' by Sean Ell

'A Practical Guide to Commercial Property Service Charges' by Rachel Garton

'A Practical Guide to Clinical Negligence – Third Edition' by Geoffrey Simpson-Scott (Geoff)

'A Practical Guide to the Rights of Grandparents in Children Proceedings – Second Edition' by Stuart Barlow

‘The Electronic Communications Code: A Practical Guide – Second Edition’ by Kerry Bretherton KC, James Castle, Mark Loveday
‘A Practical Guide to the Independent School Standards – September 2023 Edition’ by Sarah McKimm
'A Practical Guide to Estate Administration and Crypto Assets' by Richard Marshall
‘A Practical Guide to Parental Alienation in Private and Public Law Children Cases’ by Sam King QC & Frankie Shama
‘Contested Heritage – Removing Art from Land and Historic Buildings’ by Richard Harwood QC, Catherine Dobson, David Sawtell
‘The Limits of Separate Legal Personality: When Those Running a Company Can Be Held Personally Liable for Losses Caused to Third Parties Outside of the Company’ by Dr Mike Wilkinson
‘A Practical Guide to Transgender Law’ by Robin Moira White & Nicola Newbegin
‘A Practical Guide to ‘Stranded Spouses’ in Family Law’ by Mani Singh Basi
‘A Practical Guide to Residential Freehold Conveyancing’ by Lorraine Richardson
‘A Practical Guide to Pensions on Divorce for Lawyers’ by Bryan Scant
‘A Practical Guide to Challenging Sham Marriage Allegations in Immigration Law’ by Priya Solanki
‘A Practical Guide to Digital Communications Evidence in Criminal Law’ by Sam Willis
‘A Practical Guide to Legal Rights in Scotland’ by Sarah-Jane Macdonald
‘A Practical Guide to New Build Conveyancing’ by Paul Sams & Rebecca East
‘A Practical Guide to Inherited Wealth on Divorce’ by Hayley Trim
‘A Practical Guide to Practice Direction 12J and Domestic Abuse in Private Law Children Proceedings’ by Rebecca Cross & Malvika Jaganmohan
‘A Practical Guide to Confiscation and Restraint’ by Narita Bahra QC, John Carl Townsend, David Winch
‘A Practical Guide to the Law of Forests in Scotland’ by Philip Buchan
‘A Practical Guide to Health and Medical Cases in Immigration Law’ by Rebecca Chapman & Miranda Butler
‘A Practical Guide to Bad Character Evidence for Criminal Practitioners by Aparna Rao
‘A Practical Guide to Extradition Law post-Brexit’ by Myles Grandison et al
‘A Practical Guide to Hoarding and Mental Health for Housing Lawyers’ by Rachel Coyle

'Stephens on Contractual Indemnities' by Richard Stephens
'A Practical Guide to the EU Succession Regulation' by Richard Frimston
'A Practical Guide to Solicitor and Client Costs – Second Edition' by Robin Dunne
'Constructive Dismissal – Practice Pointers and Principles' by Benjimin Burgher
'A Practical Guide to Religion and Belief Discrimination Claims in the Workplace' by Kashif Ali
'A Practical Guide to the Law of Medical Treatment Decisions' by Ben Troke
'Fundamental Dishonesty and QOCS in Personal Injury Proceedings: Law and Practice' by Jake Rowley
'A Practical Guide to the Law in Relation to School Exclusions' by Charlotte Hadfield & Alice de Coverley
'A Practical Guide to Divorce for the Silver Separators' by Karin Walker
'The Right to be Forgotten – The Law and Practical Issues' by Melissa Stock
'A Practical Guide to Planning Law and Rights of Way in National Parks, the Broads and AONBs' by James Maurici QC, James Neill et al
'A Practical Guide to Election Law' by Tom Tabori
'A Practical Guide to the Law in Relation to Surrogacy' by Andrew Powell
'A Practical Guide to Claims Arising from Fatal Accidents – Second Edition' by James Patience
'A Practical Guide to Asbestos Claims' by Jonathan Owen & Gareth McAloon
'A Practical Guide to Stamp Duty Land Tax in England and Northern Ireland' by Suzanne O'Hara
'A Practical Guide to the Law of Farming Partnerships' by Philip Whitcomb
'A Practical Guide to the Law of Unlawful Eviction and Harassment – Second Edition' by Stephanie Lovegrove
'A Practical Guide to Costs in Personal Injury Claims – Second Edition' by Matthew Hoe
'A Practical Guide to the General Data Protection Regulation (GDPR) – Second Edition' by Keith Markham
'A Practical Guide to Working with Litigants in Person and McKenzie Friends in Family Cases' by Stuart Barlow
'Protecting Unregistered Brands: A Practical Guide to the Law of Passing Off' by Lorna Brazell
'A Practical Guide to Secondary Liability and Joint Enterprise Post-Jogee' by Joanne Cecil & James Mehigan

'A Practical Guide to the Pre-Action RTA Claims Protocol for Personal Injury Lawyers' by Antonia Ford
'A Practical Guide to Neighbour Disputes and the Law' by Alexander Walsh
'A Practical Guide to Coercive Control for Legal Practitioners and Victims' by Rachel Horman
'A Practical Guide to the Law of Driverless Cars – Second Edition'
by Alex Glassbrook, Emma Northey & Scarlett Milligan
'A Practical Guide to TOLATA Claims' by Greg Williams
'A Practical Guide to Elderly Law – Second Edition' by Justin Patten
'A Practical Guide to Responding to Housing Disrepair and Unfitness Claims' by Iain Wightwick
'A Practical Guide to the Law of Bullying and Harassment in the Workplace' by Philip Hyland
'How to Be a Freelance Solicitor: A Practical Guide to the SRA-Regulated Freelance Solicitor Model' by Paul Bennett
'A Practical Guide to Prison Injury Claims' by Malcolm Johnson
'A Practical Guide to Advising Clients at the Police Station' by Colin Stephen McKeown-Beaumont
'A Practical Guide to Antisocial Behaviour Injunctions – Second Edition' by Iain Wightwick
'Practical Mediation: A Guide for Mediators, Advocates, Advisers, Lawyers, and Students in Civil, Commercial, Business, Property, Workplace, and Employment Cases' by Jonathan Dingle with John Sephton
'The Mini-Pupillage Workbook' by David Boyle
'A Practical Guide to Crofting Law' by Brian Inkster
'A Practical Guide to the Law of Domain Names and Cybersquatting' by Andrew Clemson
'A Practical Guide to the Law of Gender Pay Gap Reporting' by Harini Iyengar
'NHS Whistleblowing and the Law' by Joseph England
'Employment Law and the Gig Economy' by Nigel Mackay & Annie Powell
'A Practical Guide to Noise Induced Hearing Loss (NIHL) Claims' by Andrew Mckie, Ian Skeate, Gareth McAloon
'An Introduction to Beauty Negligence Claims – A Practical Guide for the Personal Injury Practitioner' by Greg Almond
'Intercompany Agreements for Transfer Pricing Compliance' by Paul Sutton
'Zen and the Art of Mediation' by Martin Plowman
'A Practical Guide to Adoption for Family Lawyers' by Graham Pegg

'A Practical Guide to Industrial Disease Claims' by Andrew Mckie & Ian Skeate
'A Practical Guide to Conducting a Sheriff Court Proof' by Andrew Stevenson
'A Practical Guide to Vicarious Liability' by Mariel Irvine
'A Practical Guide to Applications for Landlord's Consent and Variation of Leases' by Mark Shelton
'A Practical Guide to Relief from Sanctions Post-Mitchell and Denton' by Peter Causton
'A Practical Guide to Equity Release for Advisors' by Paul Sams
'A Practical Guide to Financial Services Claims' by Chris Hegarty
'A Practical Guide to Financial Ombudsman Service Claims' by Adam Temple & Robert Scrivenor
'A Practical Guide to Running Housing Disrepair and Cavity Wall Claims – Second Edition' by Andrew Mckie & Ian Skeate
'A Practical Guide to Holiday Sickness Claims – Second Edition' by Andrew Mckie & Ian Skeate
'Arguments and Tactics for Personal Injury and Clinical Negligence Claims' by Dorian Williams
'A Practical Guide to Drone Law' by Rufus Ballaster, Andrew Firman, Eleanor Clot
'On Experts: CPR35 for Lawyers and Experts' by David Boyle
'An Introduction to Personal Injury Law' by David Boyle

These books and more are available to order online direct from the publisher at www.lawbriefpublishing.com, where you can also read free sample chapters. For any queries, call us on 0844 587 2383 or email us at mail@lawbriefpublishing.com.

Our books are all generally in stock at www.amazon.co.uk with free next day delivery for Prime members, and at good legal bookshops such as Wildy & Sons.

We are regularly launching new books in our series of practical day-to-day practitioners' guides. Visit our website and join our free newsletter to be kept informed and to receive special offers, free chapters, etc.

You can also follow us on Twitter at www.twitter.com/lawbriefpub.

www.ingramcontent.com/pod-product-compliance
Lightning Source LLC
LaVergne TN
LVHW022309200926
848481LV00004B/1255